11/15   4/TB   2x

P9-DEY-358

BELLWOOD PUBLIC LIBRARY

3 1731 00062 3689

HOW
ON
EARTH
DO
WE
RECYCLE
PLASTIC?

Plastic miracle: in 1988, 9-year-old Sarah Elaine East became the first person to run normally after receiving a specially engineered plastic prosthesis.

HOW ON EARTH
DO WE RECYCLE
PLASTIC?

JANET POTTER D'AMATO

with

LAURA STEPHENSON CARTER

BELLWOOD PUBLIC LIBRARY

Illustrations by

JANET POTTER D'AMATO

THE MILLBROOK PRESS
Brookfield, Connecticut

The photos and charts included are courtesy of
R.G.P. Orthopedic Appliance, Inc., p. 2;
GE Plastics, p. 6;
Vinyl Institute of the Society of the Plastics Industry, Inc., p. 9;
Dow Chemical Co., pp. 10, 11;
National Polystyrene Recycling Co., p. 12;
American Iron and Steel Institute, p. 13;
The Plastic Lumber Co., p. 15;
John Goerg and the NY State Department of Environmental Conservation, p.16;
Plastic Bottle Institute, p. 19;
The Procter & Gamble Co., p. 21;
Waste Management, Inc., p. 22;
Howard Rosenthal, p. 23;
Quantum Chemical Corp., p. 25

Text copyright © 1992 by Stearn/Knudsen & Co.
Crafts copyright © 1992 by Janet Potter D'Amato and Stearn/Knudsen & Co.
All rights reserved. No part of this book may be reproduced in any form or by
any means, except for the inclusion of brief quotations in a review, without
permission in writing from the publisher.

Produced in association with **STEARN/KNUDSEN & CO.**

Printed in the United States of America
5 4 3 2 1

Library of Congress Cataloging-in-Publication Data
D'Amato, Janet.
How on earth do we recycle plastic? / written and illustrated by Janet D'Amato
with Laura S. Carter.
p.   cm.
Includes bibliographical references and index.
Summary: Discusses the environmental problems caused by the manufacture and
disposal of plastic and describes how it can be recycled.

ISBN 1-56294-143-7

1. Plastic scrap — Recycling — Juvenile literature. [1. Plastic scrap — Recycling. 2. Plastic scrap — Environmental aspects. 3. Recycling (Waste) 4. Refuse
and refuse disposal.] I. Carter, Laura S. (Laura Stephenson), 1952 - . II. Title.
TD798.D36   1992
363.72'82—dc20
91-22430 CIP AC

This book is printed on recycled paper.

CONTENTS

Recycled plastics, some from hamburger packages, are used in the floors and the interior and exterior walls of this experimental house in Pittsfield, Massachusetts. The house is a showcase for advances in plastic construction techniques.

1 HOW ON EARTH DO WE RECYCLE PLASTIC?

Plastics, Plastics Everywhere

How many things can you name that are made of plastic? Plastics are used in everything from toothbrushes, hairbrushes, pens, colored markers, toys, telephones, and computers to automobile, airplane, and satellite parts. What about the plastic packaging for our milk and soft-drink containers, and the plastic wrap that protects food and other products? You could say we live in an Age of Plastics.

What do we do with all those wonderful plastic things when we are through using them? For a long time we just threw them away. Now we are running out of places to put our garbage, so we have to learn how to *reduce* the amount of garbage we create in the first place, and to *reuse, repair,* and *recycle* as many things as we can.

Before we look at the ways we can recycle plastics, let's find out more about them.

From Billiard Balls to Soft-Drink Bottles

John Wesley Hyatt, a printer in Albany, New York, was hoping to win $10,000 when he invented the first commercial plastic in 1868. He called it celluloid because it was made partly of cellulose. Cellulose is the main substance in the woody part of plants and trees.

He had entered a contest to invent a cheaper substitute for the ivory used in billiard balls. Billiards was a popular game in the

1800s and is still played in many countries today. It is similar to pool: in both games, you use a long stick (a cue) to hit hard balls on a special table covered with green felt.

Hyatt did not win the contest because it was over by the time he invented celluloid billiard balls. They were not very popular anyway, because they behaved unpredictably and caught fire easily. In one saloon, a player accidentally set a ball on fire with a lit cigar. The explosion so startled everyone that the men all drew their guns. It was not until the 1920s that a new type of plastic billiard ball was created that gradually replaced the ivory balls.

Although Hyatt did not get rich from his invention, his factories made other things from celluloid, including great false teeth. Celluloid was also used for automobile curtains, combs, brush handles, and later for photographic film, which was important in the development of the movie industry. Hyatt's invention changed the world.

In 1909, Leo H. Baekeland tried to develop a synthetic shellac by mixing some chemicals together. Imagine his surprise when instead of a syrupy liquid, he discovered a rocklike substance that he could not remove from his test tube. It became known as Bakelite in honor of its inventor, and it is still used in such items as television cabinets and telephones.

In 1938, chemists at Du Pont produced nylon, the first all-synthetic plastic that could be spun into fibers for making cloth. By 1940, nylon was being turned into toothbrush bristles, fishing line, and 64 million pairs of women's stockings! Today, nylon is used in a great many things, but most frequently in textiles.

During the 50s, 60s, and 70s, chemists in Germany, Great Britain, and the United States invented new kinds of plastics. These plastics are made from the elements found in nature: petroleum, natural gas, and coal. Basic compounds—carbon, hydrogen, oxygen, and nitrogen—are extracted from these materials, then mixed in different combinations. Using heat, pressure, or chemical action, they can then be transformed into new materials that never existed before.

Plastic bottles were introduced during the 1970s, and they quickly replaced reusable glass. By 1976, plastic had overtaken steel as the most widely used material in the United States.

Back in 1938, about 190,000 pounds of plastic were being made; today, 60 billion pounds are produced each year worldwide. By the year 2001, experts predict that over 100 billion pounds of plastics a year will be produced on earth. That would be the same as about 8 million elephants!

Vinyl plastic bottles can be recycled into pipe fencing, industrial tiles, and other useful products.

Popular Plastics

It's easy to see why plastics have become so popular. They are lightweight, durable, and often unbreakable. They can be transformed into many different shapes, forms, and colors. Plastic packaging keeps food fresher on supermarket shelves and protects against contamination. Many products that were once packaged in glass—peanut butter, shampoo, soft-drinks—are now safer to handle. If you drop a plastic bottle on the hard bathroom floor, you don't have to worry about getting a glass sliver in your foot!

Before plastics, eyeglass lenses, tennis rackets, toothpaste tubes, cups, plates, even drinking glasses all used to be made from other materials. Can you think of more things to add to this list?

In medicine, plastics are already being used to make artificial limbs and artificial heart valves. Doctors predict that some day people's lives may be saved by plastic hearts or other plastic organs.

Plastics are valuable to the transportation and aerospace industries, too. Lightweight plastic parts have replaced heavier materials like steel. Lighter cars and airplanes are now more fuel-efficient. And because of plastics, it is easier to launch lighter satellites into space, using less fuel.

There seems to be no limit to what may be manufactured from plastics. Back in 1979, an experimental racing car drove several hundred miles using an engine made of plastic. In the future, we may live in plastic houses and drive cars made only of plastic. Someday, we might even see climate-controlled cities under plastic domes or people living in plastic satellites that orbit the earth.

In 1988, James Worden, a Massachusetts Institute of Technology student, designed this solar-energy racing car. Because it is made of lightweight plastic material, it can go at high speed and for longer distances than its competitors.

There is not enough landfill space to put our ever-growing mountains of garbage.

Too Much Garbage

Although plastics are helpful in many ways, they can also be a problem. The main one is that they are very hard to get rid of.

Improperly discarded plastics can hurt wildlife. Birds, fish, and wild animals choke on plastic that they mistake for food. Animals have been known to strangle on six-pack rings. (In 1990, 34,722 six-pack rings were picked up from United States beaches!) Plastic fishing nets and lines often get lost in the ocean, snaring fish and other marine life.

The process of manufacturing plastics uses our limited natural resources and releases pollutants into the environment. But plastics are only a part of the whole problem of garbage.

11

Suppose you had lived during the 1800s. You might have gone to the store with your parents to buy food and other goods. Everything was sold in bulk. If you wanted to buy sugar, the clerk would scoop it out of a huge barrel and put it in a bag or container that you had brought to the store with you. And liquids, such as molasses or vinegar, would be kept in big kegs. The clerk would fill your own bottle or jug for you.

So much has happened in our century. New refrigeration systems meant that food could be transported and stored more easily. In the 1930s, self-service supermarkets started to become popular. Customers liked being able to look over the shelves without being interrupted by sales clerks. Soon other types of self-service stores followed: drugstores, hardware and variety stores.

Packaging became more important as high-speed machinery was invented to handle and package every kind of product. It not only kept products neat and fresh, but it had to be attractive enough to catch the customer's eye. Now packaging rather than persuasive sales clerks sell the products.

Today, life is so fast-paced that people like to save time whenever they can. The fast-food industry is growing, because so many of us want convenient take-home meals. Supermarkets offer specially packaged food that is quick and easy to prepare. Since three out of four households use microwave ovens, microwaveable products are in demand. Most of these convenience foods have one thing in common: plastic packaging.

Plastic foam products can be recycled into new items, such as waste containers, flower pots, and insulation.

Many products are deliberately made to wear out or to be replaced in a relatively short time. Clothing is designed to go out of style. The cost of repairing a broken appliance may be greater than the cost of buying a new one. We have become a "throwaway" society—and we are running out of places to throw our garbage. Keep track of how much trash you and your family throw away during a week. You will be shocked to find that each of you probably throws out at least one large garbage can of trash a week! And many of the items you throw away are made of plastic.

In fact, the United States, generates 160 million tons of garbage a year, which means that each of us produces about three and a half pounds of garbage a day. Plastics make up less than 10 percent by weight but about 20 percent by volume of what is thrown into the garbage. Most of that is packaging. Unless something is done to solve the garbage problem, our country will soon be producing 190 million tons of garbage a year. That amount of garbage would weigh more than 30 million elephants!

More and more communities and businesses are providing drop-off or buy-back centers where people can return recyclables.

Landfills. At present, our garbage is likely to end up in a sanitary landfill, or at an incinerator where it is burned. Some towns may collect garbage from people's homes, while in other areas people have to take their garbage to the landfills themselves. In some parts of the country where people live too far away from landfills, they burn some of their garbage and take the rest to the dump.

In a sanitary landfill, bulldozers spread trash out and compact it into a thin layer, then cover it with earth. More layers of trash and dirt are added. Years later, when the landfill is full, it is covered over with earth and turned into a recreational area like a park, a golf course, or even a ski area.

But some of the trash in landfills contains dangerous substances that can seep into the ground and pollute our water supply. Newer landfills have been built with a combination of clay and plastic liners that are designed to keep such hazardous materials from escaping.

There are other problems with landfills. As garbage decomposes, or rots, it smells bad and produces a colorless, odorless, explosive gas called methane. But not all the garbage rots. Garbage that is buried deep in a landfill does not get enough air to decompose naturally. Scientists who have studied landfills have found 40-year-old newspapers that are still readable. They have even come across decades-old hot dogs. Plastics may not decompose at all. A plastic container could stay around for more than 500 years!

Finally, our landfills are filling up fast. In fact, 14,000 of America's 20,000 landfills closed between 1978 and 1988. By 1993, another 2,000 are expected to close. It is getting harder to find places for new ones, because people do not want to live near a landfill. That's called the NIMBY syndrome: Not In My BackYard.

Degradable Plastics. You may have heard about plastics that are "degradable." That means they are supposed to decompose, or break down. The problem is that most degradable plastic only breaks down into smaller pieces of plastic. So a degradable plastic garbage bag ends up as thousands of tiny pieces instead of one big bag. The amount of plastic is the same—it is just in smaller pieces.

There are different types of degradable plastics. Photo-degradable plastics break down when they are exposed to sunlight. The problem is that in landfills, the plastics are buried and do not get any sunlight.

Biodegradable plastics are made partly of cornstarch. Bacteria eat the cornstarch; then other chemicals are supposed to break down the rest of the plastic into smaller pieces. But the remaining plastic may never be exposed to the chemicals that are supposed to break them down.

Some plastics are completely degradable—for example, surgical thread and the protective coverings used for the roots of seedlings. But these plastics are very expensive, and unlikely to be used for ordinary garbage bags or other things we might throw away.

The plastics industry is trying to create new materials that will decompose, but experts are worried that the decomposing process could release toxic substances from the plastics into the ground and water. And even if they do become safe, plastics will still take up space in a landfill.

Last, you should know that usually degradable plastics cannot be mixed with recyclable plastics. What do you think would happen to a park bench made of recycled plastics that had been contaminated with degradable plastics?

Benches and playground equipment can be made from 100 percent recycled nondegradable plastic lumber.

Incinerators. Instead of being put in landfills, some trash is burned in large furnaces called incinerators. The first incinerator in the United States was built in 1885 on Governor's Island in New York. In 1991, there were about 170 incinerators in the United States, with 19 more being built in 1992.

Specially designed incinerators, known as "resource recovery" plants, can burn garbage for fuel. The heat is converted into steam, which can then be used to generate electricity, to heat and cool buildings, and even to power the incinerator itself.

Incinerators help us to get rid of trash, and may produce useful energy in the process, but they can also cause pollution problems. Even though the incinerators have equipment to control pollution, some toxins are released into the air as the garbage burns. When some plastics and certain other materials are burned, the ash that remains afterwards may be considered dangerous waste that cannot be put into a regular landfill.

Garbage is transported to a waste-to-energy incinerator in Peekskill, New York.

The Solutions

Reducing. What can we do to help reduce the amount of garbage being created? We can cut down on the number of things we purchase in the first place. We can avoid excessively packaged goods, and not bring home plastic containers and bags we don't need. We can also reuse, repair, and recycle things instead of just throwing them out.

Next time you are in the supermarket, take a look at the packaging. Some of it is necessary to keep products like food and medication fresh and to prevent tampering. But most of that extra packaging is to make the product look more attractive so you will buy it. Did you know that $1 out of every $11 Americans spend on food and beverages goes for the packaging?

Some plastics manufacturers are working to reduce the amount of plastic in their containers. Designers and marketers are trying to find ways to cut down on packaging and to design their products with recycling in mind. They are not only responding to people's concerns about the environment, they are hoping to save money too.

You might think that one good way to reduce the amount of plastic you use is to carry goods home from the store in a paper bag instead of a plastic one. To a degree, this is true. However, to make paper, many trees that provide shelter for wildlife are destroyed. And papermaking contributes to air and water pollution, just as plastics manufacturing does. This is why a reusable canvas bag would be an even better solution than trading plastic for paper. At least paper comes from a renewable resource: trees. Plastics rely on a nonrenewable resource: oil.

Reusing and Repairing. Many people are substituting reusable products for disposable ones. Instead of throwaways, they purchase razors with replaceable blades and pens that are refillable. They are switching from disposable to cloth diapers.

At the Mountain Parks School in Berkeley Heights, New Jersey, sixth-grade students, in their Help Our World (HOW) project, teach younger students about packing "environmental lunches." They recommend using lunch boxes, or making lunch bags out of old bluejeans or lined plastic bags. Instead of plastic sandwich bags, they suggest using reusable plastic containers or plastic produce bags from the grocery store. And they tell the younger children to use thermoses instead of buying drinks in juice boxes.

There are lots of ways that you, too, can reuse plastic, especially the plastic food containers that come from the grocery store or delicatessen (see What You Can Do, p. 23, and Part 2, p. 26, for suggestions).

Another way of preventing waste is to select well-made products that won't break easily. But if something does break, see if you can get it repaired. Save parts from one broken toy to fix another.

Recycling. In 1989, fourth graders at the Silver Lake Elementary School, in Bladen, Nebraska, began their "Recycle 1,000" project by collecting 1,000 plastic milk jugs for recycling. Pretty soon the whole school was involved, and in ten months 112 students had collected 3,000 plastic milk jugs!

Recycling is the process of collecting, sorting, and processing recyclable items to be used again, either in their original form or as raw material in making new products. When we recycle, we are helping to preserve the environment, and we save natural resources such as trees and fuels.

A community can save money when it recycles because it does not have to take so much waste to a landfill or incinerator. Selling recyclable materials may pay for the costs associated with a recycling program. And recycling can also help the economy of a local community by creating jobs in a recycling program or processing center.

In 1990, less than one percent of plastics were recycled. But the plastics industry was starting to improve. It developed a system of package coding that identifies seven different types of plastics. If you look on the bottom of a plastic container, you may find a number stamped inside a triangle. This identification system helps in the recycling process, because the plastic items can be sorted according to type.

Plastic Container Code System for Plastic Bottles

	CODE	MATERIAL	TYPICAL PRODUCTS
⟨1⟩	PETE	Polyethylene terephthalate (PET)	soft-drink bottles
⟨2⟩	HDPE	High-density polyethylene	milk jugs, laundry detergent
⟨3⟩	V	Vinyl/polyvinyl chloride (PVC)	vegetable oil bottles
⟨4⟩	LDPE	Low-density polyethylene	dry cleaning and bread bags
⟨5⟩	PP	Polypropylene	yogurt cups
⟨6⟩	PS	Polystyrene	carry-out containers
⟨7⟩	Other	All other resins and layered multimaterial	microwaveable serving ware

At present, the plastic things most commonly recycled are soft-drink bottles made out of polyethylene terephthalate (PETE or PET), coded 1, and milk jugs, detergent bottles, and other containers made out of high-density polyethylene (HDPE), coded 2.

The plastics are collected and sorted by hand or by machine at the reprocessing plant. The containers are chopped up into flakes in a high-speed grinder, cleaned with a water spray, then dried in a huge tumble dryer. The dry flakes are melted down, molded into strands, and chopped into pellets. These pellets of recycled plastic can then be used to make new products.

But it is not enough to simply collect plastics for recycling. There has to be a demand for products made of recycled plastics. In other words, people have to want to buy them. The plastics industry is trying to create recycled products that people can use.

What kinds of things can recycled plastics be made into? Soft-drink bottles, coded 1, can be remade into other bottles, skis, surfboards, the polyester filling for sleeping bags, carpeting, pillows, even quilted jackets. Plastic milk jugs and other containers, coded 2, can be made into toys, flower pots, automobile parts, piping, bags, crates, and bottles.

Polystyrene, coded 6, which is used in foam cups and carry-out containers from fast-food restaurants, can be recycled into office supplies like pens, rulers, and trays, as well as video tape cases. These and other types of plastics can be made into picnic tables, park benches, playground equipment, and fencing.

Manufacturing companies in America are experimenting with new methods of recycling plastics. The Procter & Gamble Company, working with the Plastics Recycling Foundation, developed the first technology to make bottles out of 100 percent recycled plastic. These bottles are made from PET plastic and used for household cleaning products.

The Government. The Environmental Protection Agency (EPA) is the federal government agency that enforces the laws protecting the environment. It has set the goal of recycling 25 percent of our garbage by 1992. In 1990, just 10 percent of the garbage we produced was being recycled; 80 percent was being put into landfills, and the other 10 percent into incinerators. Some local governments have set even higher recycling goals than what the EPA recommends.

In 1991, at least 30 states had laws requiring that standardized codes be stamped onto plastic bottles so they could be sorted for recycling. Some local governments have even passed laws that either ban or sharply curb the use of some kinds of plastic.

Industry and Business. In 1988, a group of companies in the plastics industry got together to develop realistic standards for the safe disposal and recycling of plastics. They founded the Council for Solid Waste Solutions.

The Council helps to get new solid waste management technologies from the designing board to the production line. To put these solutions into practice, it works with local, state, and federal officials, as well as community and environmental organizations. The Council's goal is to make plastics one of the most recycled materials by the year 2000.

Du Pont and other plastics-manufacturing companies are recycling their industrial plant waste. In 1990, more than one million pounds of clear plastic filament (thread), normally considered waste at the factory, was recycled into other industrial products.

Companies, large and small, are recycling paper, aluminum, and plastics. Some supermarkets even recycle plastic bags or sell canvas bags that can be used and reused to carry home groceries. Convenience stores like 7-Eleven are selling soft-drinks and coffee in reusable plastic cups and glasses.

Plastic foam packing pieces protect fragile items during shipment. Some packaging services provide drop-off boxes where consumers can return them for recycling.

In 1990, Procter & Gamble introduced paper-based packets of concentrated liquid fabric softener for refilling plastic containers that people can keep at home. The Eastman Kodak Company, on a test basis, has started recycling its plastic film containers and disposable cameras. McDonald's plans to use recycled construction materials and has stopped using plastic foam hamburger boxes. Beverage companies are designing six-pack rings that can be snapped apart and will melt in sunlight.

Pearlridge Elementary School children in Oahu, Hawaii, are rewarded for their recycling efforts.

Communities. All across the nation, towns and cities are recycling plastics and other materials. At least nine states have passed laws requiring communities to provide curbside pick-up of recyclable materials. In other communities, residents may take their recyclables to recycling centers.

Groups like the Girl Scouts and the Boy Scouts of America organize clean-up days, when people help to clean up beaches, roadsides, parks, and other public areas.

Students at the Ocean City Elementary School in Maryland started a program called "Students Tackle Ocean Plastic" (STOP). They teach the public about the dangers of plastics in the ocean, organize a beach clean-up each year, and are committed to destroying the plastic six-pack rings that they find.

Many organizations, such as the National Audubon Society, offer environmental education programs for children as well as adults. To find out what's available to you, check the sources listed at the back of this book (under Find Out More) and your state, city, and local government agencies and environmental organizations.

What You Can Do

If you look around your community, you can probably find people who have discovered interesting ways to reuse and recycle plastics.

A sculptor in New York City creates birdcages and aquariums out of old plastic television cabinets.

In Nevada, a scientist gives his empty yogurt containers to researchers at a university greenhouse to use for new plant seedlings. He also reuses plastic bags when he is collecting things on natural history field trips.

Sculptor Howard Rosenthal turned a discarded TV set into an imaginative birdcage.

A West Milford, New Jersey, high school student protested the use of polystyrene trays in the school cafeteria. Out of her effort grew an environmental club which convinced the board of education to start a recycling program in the township schools and to co-sponsor state recycling legislation.

Thousands of people are doing what they can to solve the garbage problem and to help save our environment. Here's a list of ideas to get you started. You will probably want to add some of your own.

1. Keep used bags in a "bag of bags" handy at the door to remind your family to take a few when they go shopping, so they won't need new ones at the store. Also use cloth bags or backpacks.

2. When shopping, buy those plastic items that are already marked with coded numbers (see chart, p. 19) of the plastics being recycled in your community.

3. When shopping with your family, suggest that they don't buy disposable pens, razors, cameras, plates, and flatware made of plastics, but find long-lasting products.

4. During "show and tell," bring in samples of different packaging and explain the advantages and disadvantages of each.

5. Start a Barter Day at school to trade items with each other for reuse. Or have a "grab bag" party with used or outgrown toys (in good condition, of course).

6. At home or school, start a letter-writing campaign to encourage manufacturers and chain stores to reduce the amount of packaging for their products. They are influenced by what consumers think.

7. Keep informed about recycling programs in your community, and get your friends, family, and school to participate. Use your telephone directory and library reference section to locate participating businesses and government agencies.

8. See if your supermarket or dry cleaner will take back used plastic bags. (The A&P and ShopRite stores do.)

9. Reuse plastic containers—they're great for starting new plants, or storing small toy parts or leftover food.

10. Write letters about recycling to the editor of your local newspaper, and to local, state, and federal government officials.

11. Get involved with environmental organizations.

12. Be a crafts recycler. Now turn to the second part of this book to explore the creative world of plastic crafts.

Recycled plastic milk bottles make safe nests for wood ducks.

2 CRAFT IT!

Making a craft is a creative and fun way to reuse plastic discards. The ideas that follow show some of the many possible uses of plastics to make school projects, toys, gifts, ornaments, constructions, and decorations. Gather and save all sorts of plastic items usually thrown out with the garbage. Wash bottles and containers and soak off the labels. You will soon acquire a treasure box of materials to be retrieved and recycled whenever you work on crafts projects. Check with an adult before bringing home any discards from public places. You may see an interesting object you might use, but never, NEVER reach into a public trash container of any kind. You could get a dangerous cut or infection. And never push or try to compact items into a public trash bin. If you need a lot of a certain discard such as straws, collect them from friends as you finish lunch at school. Wash them. Get together with friends to save discards and trade what you need for your particular project.

Tools. Most kinds of plastic can be cut with scissors. Heavier ones may need a knife. Let an adult do that cutting for you. (See Plastic Bottles, p. 30. For cutting polystyrene, plastic foam sometimes called Styrofoam, see Constructions and Styrostructures, p. 38.) To make holes in plastic, use an awl (or nutpick, ice pick, or sharp nail). The awl might not penetrate a heavy plastic. With adult supervision, heat the tip of the awl in a candle flame. Push the heated tip through the plastic to make the hole. (If using a nail, hold it with pliers.) Some holes can be made with a paper punch. Otherwise, few tools will be needed. Assuming you have a pencil, ruler, and scissors on hand, these will not be listed under "Materials."

Gluing and Assembling. As there are so many kinds of plastics, it is difficult to suggest one brand of glue. Some glues work fine on one plastic, but not on others. Avoid those that are flammable (catch fire easily) or have heavy fumes. Most need to be used in a well-ventilated area. Always follow label instructions. White glue is best for general use and is the safest. When the instructions say, "Glue," try this kind first. You may be able to use some glue left over from plastic modelmaking (follow the precautions on the label carefully). Sometimes the glue will hold better if the surface is roughened with sandpaper. Other methods of attaching pieces are discussed under the Sculpture project (see p. 53).

Paints. Spray-on paints made for plastic models can be purchased in a hobby store. Read and follow the precautions on the label. Acrylic (from an art or hobby store) or leftover latex household paint will work on most plastics and can be thinned and cleaned up with water. Be sure to clean brushes immediately. Once acrylic dries, it is permanent. Poster paint will work on some plastic, but it is not permanent. Color or details can be added with permanent markers. If paint does not stick well, add a few drops of liquid detergent. On a problem surface, it may help to sand it lightly before painting.

Finishing. To hide the humble origins of your crafts, consider buying some new materials: ribbons, gold braid, rickrack, and other trimmings. Use colored paper, tissue paper, picture cut-outs, yarn, and felt, as well as paint, to make your creations attractive. Stickers are a quick way to add design and color. Adhesive-backed vinyl (such as Contact) comes in many colors and textures. Use leftovers or buy some new pieces for a special project. On the other hand, if you want a "Now" or futuristic look—unadorned plastic is great. Make the most of it.

   The following chart will give you some ideas for using plastic discards found in your home.

PLASTIC RECYCLING IDEAS

DISCARDS	SOURCES & NOTES	SUGGESTED REUSES
Bags: bread, shopping, dry cleaner, etc.	Lightweight plastic	Storage, stuffing, packing; cut open & use to cover work surfaces, for temporary apron or bib
Balloons	Mylar: attach with rubber cement	Colorful additions: art, mobiles, constructions, greeting cards
Beads: discarded jewelry	Much costume jewelry is plastic	Ornaments, new jewelry from old parts, dollhouse accessories, art, assemblages
Berry baskets		Snowflake ornaments of cut sections; protect bows in shipping, assemblages
Blister packing	Remove card backing	Ornaments (see Holiday Decorations); covering small collectibles, photo frame
Bottles: soda, bleach, cosmetic, detergent	Clean, soak off labels	(See Plastic Bottles) Toys, masks, puppets, door stop (fill with sand), plant pot, terrarium, assemblages, sculptures
Buttons	Most are now plastic	Dollhouse accessories, eyes for toy animals, jewelry, art
Box inserts	Thin molded shapes around cookies, candy	Sort and keep small items; show off collectibles, assemblages, constructions
Caps and tops	From bottles, jars, spray cans, cosmetics, etc.	Bases (fill with plaster), checkers, playing pieces, coasters, ornaments (see Holiday Decorations), mobiles, art, constructions
Clear wrap		Doll raincoat, bookcover; keep hobby specimens, wrap paintbrushes
Containers: margarine tub, food, deli, pantyhose egg	Clean thoroughly	(See Containers and Egg Cartons) Storage, tom-tom, plant pots, decorate for gifts, constructions, mixing and storing paint
Cups	Disposable plastic foam	Bells, string holder; cut to make decorations, assemblages, constructions
Egg cartons	Plastic	Seed starters, extra ice cube tray, game (Mankala), constructions
Fishing line (nylon mono-filament)	When tangled, cut into lengths	Mobiles, hanging loops for ornaments, art, constructions

DISCARDS	SOURCES & NOTES	SUGGESTED REUSES
Garden hose	Cut useless hose in lengths	Door bumper, replace lost bicycle handles, pail handle, constructions
Glasses: clear, disposable	Plastic party ware	(See Constructions) Storage, ornaments, assemblages
Lids	From containers	Photo frames, coasters, assemblages, mobiles, art
Meat and produce trays: plastic foam	From supermarket; clean	Toys, little planes (use instead of balsawood), constructions, art, paint palette, mobiles
Net bags	From onions, turkey, etc.	Storage, coverings, decorations, art, collages
Packing "peanuts"	Used to protect items in shipping	Decorations, stuffing, art
Panty hose	Nylon; wash	Strainer for paint, stuffing, soft sculpture, soft toys, weaving strips for rugs
Picnic discards: spoons, plates	Clean	Note holder, puppet heads, art, assemblages
Pill bottles	Clean	Store small items; dollhouse dishes (caps), assemblages
Polyester fiberfill	Old pillows	Stuffing for soft toys, beard on stuffed Santa
Polystyrene packing corners	Plastic foam, such as Styrofoam	(See Constructions) Great for large structures, sculpture, projects, dioramas
Spools: sewing thread	Once wood, now plastic	Toys, chess pieces, constructions, base of dollhouse table
Straws (drinking)	Clean	Lengthen flower stems in arranging, mobiles, constructions
Toothbrushes	Clean	Splatter painting, stencil brush; use to clean small areas; assemblages
Vinyl: table-cloths, shower curtains, old plastic raincoats, imitation leather		Bib, apron, rain scarf, bookcover, placemats cut from old tablecloths; make a shopping bag, stuffed toys; protect work areas; cover outdoor furniture

PLASTIC BOTTLES

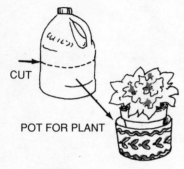

CUT

POT FOR PLANT

Your family and community discard countless plastic bottles daily. You can do many interesting things with these bottles.

Clean out the bottles and soak off the labels. Some smaller bottles may be cut with a scissors. The larger bottles (laundry, detergent, bleach, etc.) are thick and difficult to cut. Do not attempt to cut them yourself. Place the bottle on a steady table. Ask an adult to do the basic cutting with a mat, or utility, knife. Then, using a large, sturdy scissors, you may be able to complete the cutting. Always be extremely careful when using a cutting tool.

You can make a funnel, soap dish, or wall caddy by cutting off the lower section of a bottle and then decorating it. Put a potted plant in a bottle bottom.

A diagonally cut bottle makes a scoop for salt or sand in winter, fertilizer in spring. For summer, cut various-shaped bottles to use in making sandcastles.

To make a pencil caddy, cut, poke holes, and thread a plastic lanyard, lacing around the top to decorate it. Add colorful stickers.

Remove the extra base of a soda bottle. Cut and invert the bottle into a jar cap for a dome to display a collectible.

Make a bird feeder: Cut a hole in a gallon-sized bottle. Poke a small hole below and insert a straw or dowel, going through to the other side. Punch a hole in the cap. Tie a knot in the end of a piece of cord. Thread the cord through the hole, replace the cap, and hang it up.

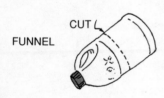

SOAP DISH

CUT

3"-4" DIAMETER

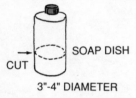

CUT

FUNNEL

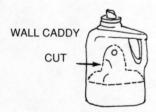

WALL CADDY

CUT

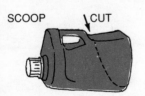

SCOOP   CUT

PENCIL CADDY

END OF
SODA BOTTLE

CAP

DISPLAY DOME

BIRD FEEDER

BOTTLE FIGURES: TRADITIONAL DOLL

Empty mouthwash bottles, dish detergent, shampoo, and syrup containers can be transformed into all sorts of characters. Add arms and a head to the bottle. Then use your imagination to dress and decorate it.

MATERIALS

- Bottle
- Yarn
- Panty hose
- 1/4 yd cotton fabric (or discarded blouse)
- 1 1/2" plastic foam ball (2" for larger bottle)
- Two chenille stems (or pipe cleaners or wire)
- 1/2" wide ribbon
- Needle and thread
- Paper for patterns

INSTRUCTIONS

1. For arms and to attach head, make holes with awl near neck of bottle.

2. Push end of one chenille stem through the hole, up out of the neck, through head ball. Twist end at top. Slide other arm into the other hole, twist together at neck. Pull out on arms so head sets firmly on neck.

3. Bend up chenille stems to make arms about 4 1/2" long. Twist at elbow and wrist.

4. Stretch a piece of panty hose around the head. Tie in back, trim off excess.

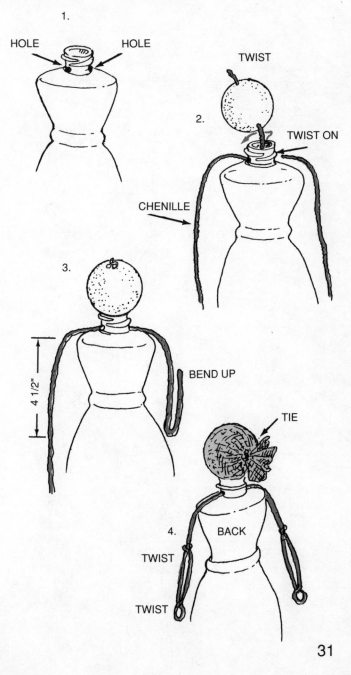

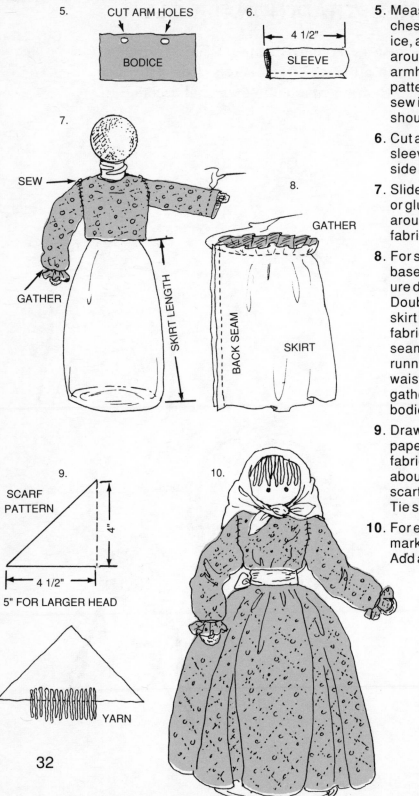

5. CUT ARM HOLES

BODICE

6. 4 1/2"

SLEEVE

7. SEW

GATHER

SKIRT LENGTH

8. GATHER

BACK SEAM

SKIRT

9. SCARF PATTERN

4"

4 1/2"

5" FOR LARGER HEAD

YARN

10.

5. Measure circumference of bottle at chest. Draw paper pattern for bodice, as shown. Add 1/2" overlap. Fit around bottle to check size. Mark armholes. Adjust as needed. Trace pattern on fabric and cut. Glue or sew in position, fitting in at waist and shoulders.

6. Cut a 4" x 4" piece of fabric for each sleeve. Sew up seams, turn right side out.

7. Slide a sleeve over each arm. Sew or glue to each shoulder. Tie thread around each wrist, gathering in fabric.

8. For skirt length, measure waist to base, then add 1/2" for seam. Measure distance around base of bottle. Double that measure to determine skirt fullness. Mark dimensions on fabric and cut out. Sew up back seam and turn right side out. With running stitch, make gathers at waist. Slide skirt on bottle and pull gathers tight. Knot and sew skirt to bodice.

9. Draw pattern for scarf on folded paper. Cut, open out. Cut out of fabric. Cut several pieces of yarn about 2" long. Sew to center of scarf, leaving about 1" over edge. Tie scarf on head.

10. For eyes, draw two dots with a marker. Keep eyes low on head. Add a ribbon sash.

32

VARIATIONS

Creatures made of bottles can be as weird as you wish: spacemen, monsters, space aliens, or clowns. The construction is basically the same. Use a discarded doll's head or imaginative heads (see illustrations). Instead of fabric and clothes, decorate with bright stickers and colored tapes. Slide tubes or straw on for arms. Clothes could be taped-on crepe paper for party decorations.

A bottle with a handle looks like one arm is akimbo. Work it into your creation. The one shown has stripes made from stick-on tape. The jacket, including the straw arm, is spray-painted on. Parts not to be painted are masked off. A small container becomes a hat.

Use your imagination. How many arms does your space alien have?

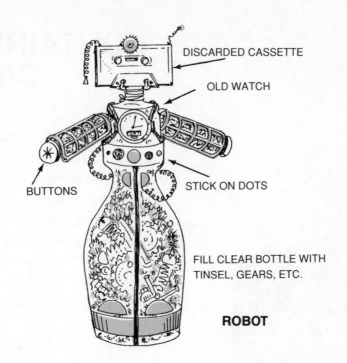

DISCARDED CASSETTE

OLD WATCH

BUTTONS

STICK ON DOTS

FILL CLEAR BOTTLE WITH TINSEL, GEARS, ETC.

ROBOT

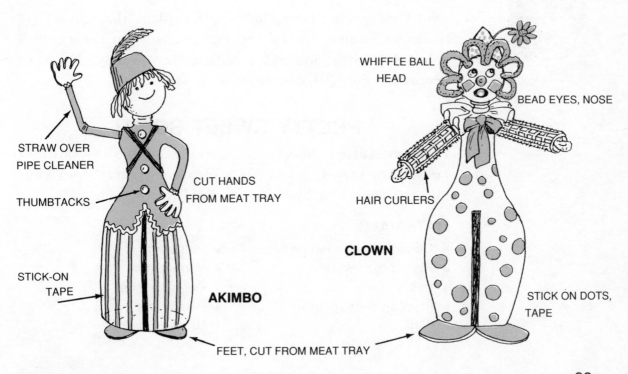

STRAW OVER PIPE CLEANER

THUMBTACKS

CUT HANDS FROM MEAT TRAY

STICK-ON TAPE

AKIMBO

FEET, CUT FROM MEAT TRAY

WHIFFLE BALL HEAD

BEAD EYES, NOSE

HAIR CURLERS

CLOWN

STICK ON DOTS, TAPE

CONTAINERS AND EGG CARTONS

Clear and colored containers of different sizes come from food products, such as margarine, cottage cheese, yogurt, deli foods, and so on. Many have snap-on lids. Some manufacturers make their containers extremely attractive, expecting you to reuse them.

Margarine tubs are good for storing leftover food, freezing small portions, or taking food for lunches and picnics. Keep your leftover paint soft in plastic containers. Clear containers are especially useful for storing things.

NET

ADD BOW

Container lids are also useful. Put them under things that drip—a can of paint, a potted plant—or use them as coasters.

When giving home-baked gifts, place them in an attractive container. Stack several together, put them into a colorful net bag, and add a ribbon. Or you may choose to decorate your gift container with stickers.

PRETTY SWEET SCENT

Potpourri (dried flowers and herbs available in craft and houseware stores) gives off a pleasant fragrance in your home. Decorate a container to hold it.

MATERIALS

- Container with snap-on lid
- Plastic egg carton
- Fabric
- Plastic leaves about 1 1/4" long
- Potpourri
- Paper punch
- Paper fastener
- Plastic bag
- Narrow ribbon

INSTRUCTIONS

1. Punch holes around lid.

2. For pattern, cut a piece of plastic bag and fit around container. Tape. Trim excess even with top and bottom. Allow overlap where ends meet. Remove and use pattern to cut shape of fabric. Glue fabric around the container.

3. Use a plastic egg carton to make a flower decoration on top. Cut out one egg-cup section in the shape as shown. Attach this piece to center of lid with a paper fastener.

4. Cut petals (sizes shown) from other egg-carton cups. Glue middle-sized petals inside attached cup. The petals should overlap slightly in a flowerlike arrangement. Allow glue to dry, then add smaller petals. Glue a row of larger petals outside around attached cup. Glue leaves to base of flower.

5. Glue a ribbon around base of container and a bow near the flower. Fill container with potpourri; snap on top.

VARIATIONS

Instead of potpourri, fill with fresh cat litter. Add a lid with holes. Put in corner of a damp closet to absorb the moisture.

Make egg-carton flowers to decorate a box, a mirror, and other projects.

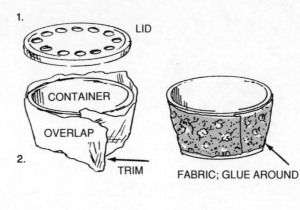

1. LID

2. CONTAINER OVERLAP TRIM FABRIC; GLUE AROUND

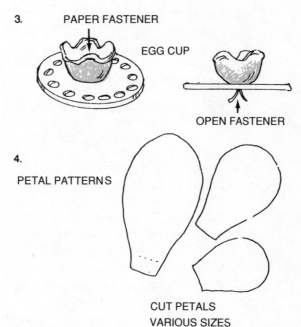

3. PAPER FASTENER EGG CUP OPEN FASTENER

4. PETAL PATTERNS

CUT PETALS VARIOUS SIZES

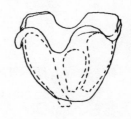

5.

PHOTO-FRAMING LIDS

MATERIALS

- Three matching lids
- Three photos
- Drinking straw
- Cord or string
- Felt
- Gold spray paint
- Rickrack
- Paper
- Compass
- Heavy needle and thread

INSTRUCTIONS

1. Paint lids if desired. Measure size of lid. With compass, draw a circle about 1/2" smaller for pattern. Lay this circle over your photo. If circle is too big, draw a smaller one on paper. Use it as a guide to cut photo into circle shape.

2. To determine size of felt backing, lay lids on felt. Plan about 1/2" on each side, 1 1/4" top and bottom. Measure and cut felt.

3. Position and sew or staple through each lid, attaching to the felt.

4. At top, glue felt around straw. Tie on a cord to hang.

5. Glue photos onto lids. Glue on rickrack trim.

ALTERNATIVE

Some thin shopping bags have plastic handles. Remove one handle from bag. Glue edge of felt to edge of handle instead of using straw.

1.

PHOTO

CUT PHOTO

2.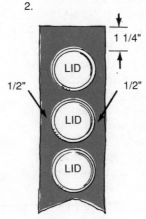

1 1/4"

1/2"   LID

1/2"

LID

LID

3.

4.

GLUE

5.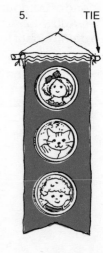

TIE

HANDLE

NOTABLE NOBODY MONSTER BANK

MATERIALS

- Container about 4" deep with lid
- Plastic foam cup
- Bread bags
- Meat tray
- Paper for patterns
- Black paper or stick-on black tape
- Stapler
- Glue

INSTRUCTIONS

1. Trace patterns (shown) on paper. Draw mouth and cut from red section of a bread bag or red paper. Cut two hands. Cut teeth out of the foam cup. Cut a foot shape about 2 1/2" long out of the meat tray.

2. For eyes, cut two 1" circles out of meat tray; cut two 1 1/8" and two 1/2" circles of black paper. Glue together as shown.

3. For legs, cut three strips from colored bread bags, 1 1/2" wide by 5 1/4" long. Braid strips. Staple one end of braid to foot, repeat for other leg.

4. Turn container over onto its base. Glue mouth to side of container. Glue teeth over mouth. Glue on eyes and attach hands beside mouth. Cut the money slot to look like a nose. Staple end of each leg to inside of container; snap lid over braids.

VARIATION

For a bird bank, make a pattern for the head and neck; include an attaching tab. Cut slot in container for tab. Cut head, wings, and tail from meat tray. Glue on head. Attach wings and tail with paper fasteners.

1.   PATTERNS

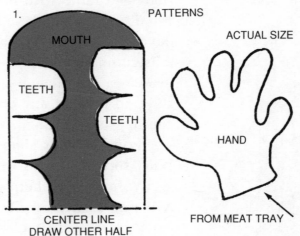

MOUTH

TEETH

TEETH

ACTUAL SIZE

HAND

CENTER LINE
DRAW OTHER HALF

FROM MEAT TRAY

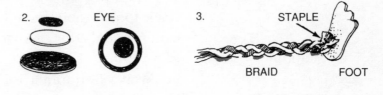

2.   EYE   3.   STAPLE

BRAID   FOOT

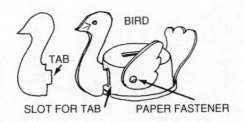

BIRD

TAB

SLOT FOR TAB   PAPER FASTENER

CONSTRUCTIONS AND STYROSTRUCTURES

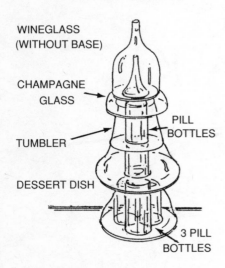

CLEAR PARTY DISCARDS

WINEGLASS (WITHOUT BASE)

CHAMPAGNE GLASS

TUMBLER

PILL BOTTLES

DESSERT DISH

3 PILL BOTTLES

DIORAMA

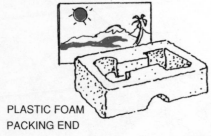

PAINT BACKGROUND

PLASTIC FOAM PACKING END

When your family buys a small appliance, there will probably be plastic foam packing shapes at both ends of the box. Never discard these packings. Their odd shapes and holes should stimulate your imagination. The foam is easily cut with a serrated knife.

Before you start cutting this polystyrene, cover the floor and table with plastic or papers. Like sawdust from wood, little crumbles of plastic are shed as you cut. They have static and fly about. If possible, work outdoors: those crumbles help to condition the soil. It's a good idea to wear a large handkerchief tied around your face, bandit-style, to prevent any crumbles getting into your nose. If a cut area is too rough, rub it across sandpaper.

Look at your shapes. How can they be recombined? What sort of project would you like to do?

Volunteer to help clean up after an adult party. You will find plenty of plastic: dishes, favors, and disposable party glasses. This clear plastic can be used just as it is. Try stacking up party ware and clear pill bottles. If the stack looks good enough to keep, then glue them together, using model glue. (*Always read and follow the advice on glue containers.*)

Make a diorama for some tiny animals. Select a base. Cut a background to fit. Whittle and cut mountains. Make a flat foreground. Add papier-mâché over the plastic foam and paint it.

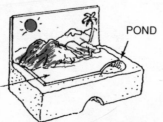

POND

PIECE OF MEAT TRAY FOR GROUND

STYRO SPACESHIP

MATERIALS

- Several large, interestingly shaped plastic foam packing pieces
- Meat trays
- Foam cups
- Straws
- Party glasses
- Nylon line, and a variety of other plastic discards
- 3" headless nails
- Toothpicks
- Paper punch
- Knife
- White glue
- Map tacks

INSTRUCTIONS

1. To plan your ship, turn, arrange, and rearrange your largest shapes of packing pieces. After deciding on the arrangement, stack them in position.

2. Some holes may be just what is needed. Or cut openings. Wherever an area is cut, edges may be rough. Cut narrow panels from meat trays to frame cut-out areas.

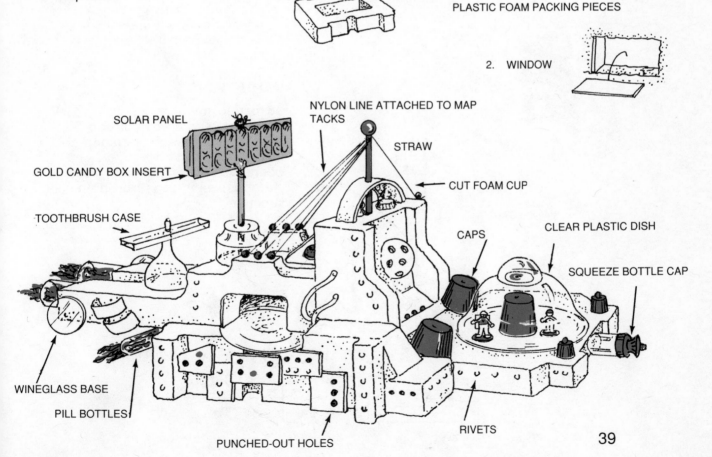

1.

PLASTIC FOAM PACKING PIECES

2. WINDOW

SOLAR PANEL

NYLON LINE ATTACHED TO MAP TACKS

STRAW

GOLD CANDY BOX INSERT

CUT FOAM CUP

TOOTHBRUSH CASE

CAPS

CLEAR PLASTIC DISH

SQUEEZE BOTTLE CAP

WINEGLASS BASE

PILL BOTTLES

PUNCHED-OUT HOLES

RIVETS

39

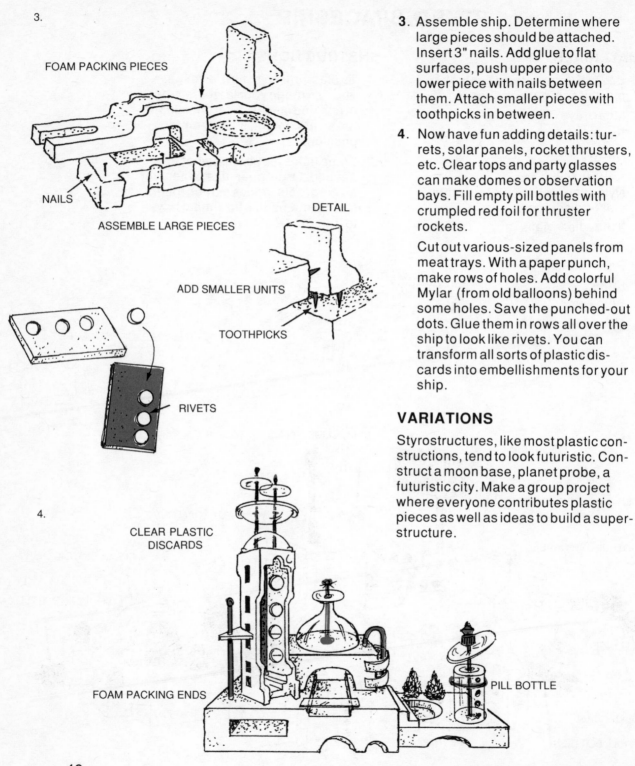

3.

FOAM PACKING PIECES

NAILS

ASSEMBLE LARGE PIECES

DETAIL

ADD SMALLER UNITS

TOOTHPICKS

RIVETS

4.

CLEAR PLASTIC DISCARDS

FOAM PACKING ENDS

PILL BOTTLE

3. Assemble ship. Determine where large pieces should be attached. Insert 3" nails. Add glue to flat surfaces, push upper piece onto lower piece with nails between them. Attach smaller pieces with toothpicks in between.

4. Now have fun adding details: turrets, solar panels, rocket thrusters, etc. Clear tops and party glasses can make domes or observation bays. Fill empty pill bottles with crumpled red foil for thruster rockets.

Cut out various-sized panels from meat trays. With a paper punch, make rows of holes. Add colorful Mylar (from old balloons) behind some holes. Save the punched-out dots. Glue them in rows all over the ship to look like rivets. You can transform all sorts of plastic discards into embellishments for your ship.

VARIATIONS

Styrostructures, like most plastic constructions, tend to look futuristic. Construct a moon base, planet probe, a futuristic city. Make a group project where everyone contributes plastic pieces as well as ideas to build a superstructure.

HISTORICAL MODELS: PUEBLO PROJECT

Maybe you prefer a castle to a moon base, or perhaps a school project calls for a model of a historical structure, such as this pueblo. Texture added over the plastic foam gives the historical or classical look.

MATERIALS

- Plastic foam packing corners
- Meat trays
- Spackle
- Sand
- Paint and brush
- Twigs
- Plastic egg
- Ice cream stick
- Rubber bands
- Clay
- Knife
- White glue

INSTRUCTIONS

1. For the base, select piece of foam about 8" x 12". Cut and glue on pieces of meat trays to make a flat ground area, covering holes.

2. Plan size and arrangement of houses. Cut several plastic foam blocks ranging in size from 7" x 4" x 3" to 3" x 2" x 2". If the plastic foam has gaps, cover with a piece of meat tray.

3. Cut door and window in each house. Assemble a block and glue together. Hold with rubber bands until glue dries. Glue houses to base and to each other. Glue half of the plastic egg to the ground to look like an outdoor oven.

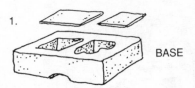

1.

BASE

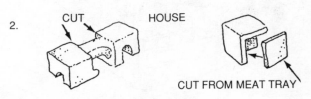

2.   CUT   HOUSE

CUT FROM MEAT TRAY

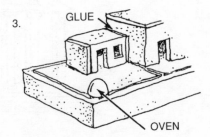

3.   GLUE

OVEN

41

4.

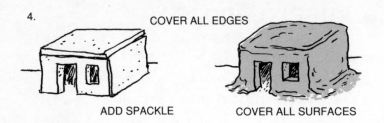

COVER ALL EDGES

ADD SPACKLE

COVER ALL SURFACES

5.

LADDER

BEAMS

FENCE

6.

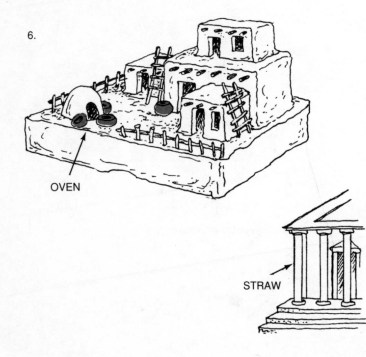

OVEN

4. You can buy a container of pre-mixed spackle. Or buy powdered spackle and mix with water into a thick paste. Using an ice-cream stick, spread spackle to make a textured ground area, covering buildings, and joinings

For the adobe look, mix tan paint in a plastic container. Add a little sand. Paint the construction. (Clean brush immediately.)

5. Natural twigs (or toothpicks) help achieve the rustic look. Make holes, insert twigs for beams and fence-posts. Glue a top rail on fence. Cut twigs and glue together for ladders.

6. Paint a door on oven. Make some tiny pots of clay and put them next to oven.

VARIATIONS

Instead of using spackle, cover with papier-mâché and paint or cover with tan clay. Almost any model can be made on a foam packing base. For adding details, use meat trays instead of balsa-wood or cardboard. Cut with a knife and use a ruler to make straight edges. Create walls, shingles, roofs, stairs, shutters—whatever is needed for your project.

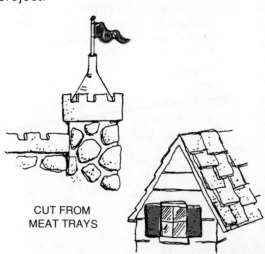

STRAW

CUT FROM
MEAT TRAYS

HOLIDAY DECORATIONS

CHRISTMAS

Recycle old ornaments and trims. String packing squiggles—just like popcorn—to decorate your tree. Space red beads between, if desired. Turn a flip-top cap into a bell tree ornament, as shown.

BLISTER ORNAMENT

When you purchase small items (screws, cosmetics, batteries), they are often covered with a plastic shape glued to a card. Transform this "blister" into Christmas ornaments.

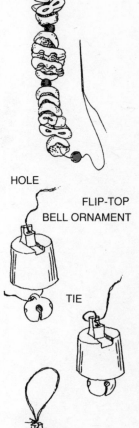

HOLE

FLIP-TOP
BELL ORNAMENT

TIE

TRIM

MATERIALS

- Blister about 3" high
- Small plastic figure (angel, reindeer, Santa) about 2" high
- Old Christmas cards
- Gold rickrack or trimming
- White glue

INSTRUCTIONS

1. Carefully remove the blister from its backing. Select Christmas card picture to go with figure. Lay blister over Christmas card. Draw around edges of blister. Cut card.

2. For the back of the ornament, from a Christmas card cut another piece the same size. Glue the two pieces together back to back.

3. Glue figure in position on card. When dry, glue blister over the card.

4. Glue rickrack or decorative edgings around on flat edge of blister to hide any printing left when it was pulled off its card. Glue a row of edging around back, as well. Tie on a hanging cord.

1.

CARD

FIGURE

BLISTER

2.

3.

4.

TREE-TRIM TOPS

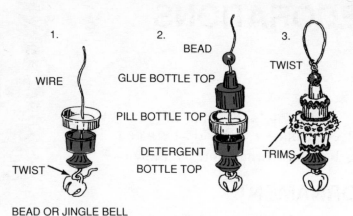

1. WIRE

TWIST

BEAD OR JINGLE BELL

2. BEAD

GLUE BOTTLE TOP

PILL BOTTLE TOP

DETERGENT BOTTLE TOP

3. TWIST

TRIMS

MATERIALS

- Two squeeze bottle tops
- Pill bottle top about 1 1/2" in diameter
- Gold trim
- Gold spray paint
- Piece of wire or pipe cleaner about 6" to 8" long
- Beads
- Jingle bell
- Glue

INSTRUCTIONS

1. Make a hole in center of pill bottle top. Insert wire through the opening in squeeze bottle top. If necessary, enlarge holes with awl or pick. Slide bead (or bell) on end of wire. Twist the end around to secure it.

2. Thread other end of wire up through caps as shown. Add bead at top.

Push together. Make a hanging loop of the wire and twist closed, tight against bead. Add glue between tops to hold them firmly against each other.

3. Spray-paint. When dry, glue on fancy braids, beads, tinsel. Add some glitter.

HANUKKAH

STAR OF DAVID ORNAMENT 1

MATERIALS

- Six plastic straws
- Plastic covered wire (like telephone wire)
- Thin nylon fishing line

INSTRUCTIONS

1. Cut all straws the same length (about 6"). Thread the wire through three straws. Bend into a triangle. Cut off wire, leaving about 3/4" at each end to twist together.

1.

2.

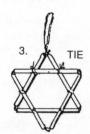

3. TIE

2. Twist together and insert ends back into straws. Repeat, making a second triangle.

3. Lay the two triangles together to form a star, as shown. Using nylon line, tie at intersecting points. Tie a hanging loop at top.

STAR OF DAVID ORNAMENT 2

MATERIALS

- Clear lid or blister
- Colored cellophane (the kind wrapped around a gift basket)
- Black marker
- Cord or narrow ribbon
- Glue
- Paper for pattern

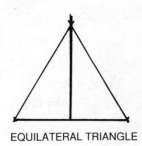

1.

WIDTH OF LID   EQUILATERAL TRIANGLE

INSTRUCTIONS

1. Make a triangle pattern on paper. Measure widest width of lid (or blister). Draw a line on paper about 1/2" less than this distance. Make a perpendicular line at center. Draw the other two sides of the triangle up to the line, each side the same length as the base line.

2. Using the pattern, cut two triangles of the colored cellophane. Over-lapped, they make a star.

3. Glue one triangle at a time to inside of lid, as shown. Press out excess glue. Wipe clean.

4. When glue is dry, turn lid over. Using a ruler, draw black lines along edges of triangles.

5. Make a hole in lid and tie on a hanging cord. If edge of plastic or blister is uneven, or if more decoration is desired, glue a cord or ribbon around it. Use the same trim at top for hanging.

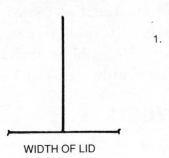

2.

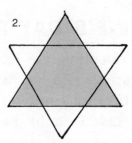

3.

4.

VARIATIONS

Cut triangles of colored tissue paper. Or draw star first; then, on reverse side of the clear plastic, fill in with colored markers.

5.

PLASTIC EGG

EASTER

Decorate old plastic eggs or a giant egg from mom's panty hose package. Cut out small pieces of old Mylar balloons, shiny ribbons. Attach to egg with rubber cement (follow the instructions on the label). Weave 3/4" ribbon through slots in a berry basket. Twist together two chenille stems and attach these for a handle.

BERRY BASKET

HALLOWEEN

Cut a pumpkin face from an orange-colored lid. Attach a string and hang it.

VALENTINE'S DAY CENTERPIECE

To make a valentine, use the thin plastic insert that once held candy inside a heart-shaped box. Cut out a backing from red posterboard. Staple plastic insert to card with lace doilies between. Fill the depressions (made to hold the chocolates) with pictures cut from old cards, plastic flowers, and little folded messages.

VALENTINE CENTERPIECE

MATERIALS

- Plastic foam packing piece about 6" long
- Red lids (4" diameter)
- Toothpicks (preferably red plastic)
- Plastic (or paper) doilies
- Red ribbon
- Heavy red paper or cards (or meat tray)
- Red or white net plastic bags

INSTRUCTIONS

1. Cover unwanted holes in the base (foam) packing piece with red card. Glue doilies around edges. Add ribbon.

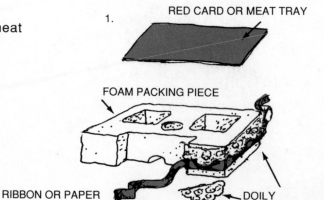

1.

RED CARD OR MEAT TRAY

FOAM PACKING PIECE

RIBBON OR PAPER   DOILY

46

2. Cut pictures from old Valentine cards. Glue picture to a card, with end of toothpick between. Let dry, then trim edges to make an attractive shape.

3. Make a heart-shaped pattern. Cut out hearts from red lids. Poke two holes in hearts. Push toothpicks through.

4. Cut the rim from the remaining piece of lid and cut it in halves.

5. To assemble: Make holes around top edge of foam and insert ends of rims to create a fence look. Poke the picks from the pictures and hearts into the foam and red paper. In between these, bunch the net and stick toothpicks through and into base. Puff up the net. Add plastic flowers on toothpicks. Tie bows, glue to end of toothpicks, and add to the centerpiece.

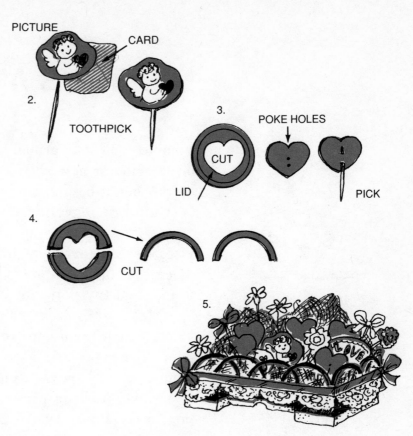

ANY OCCASION

Make centerpieces for other holidays and special occasions (wedding, birthday, new baby, etc.). Gather a variety of elements and assemble by inserting toothpicks into decorated foam. Or create an appropriate character to brighten your table. (See Bottle Figures, p. 31.)

THANKSGIVING   HALLOWEEN   WEDDING   CHRISTMAS

TOYS AND GAMES

TOSS GAME

BOWLING

Your toy chest is probably full of plastic pieces. Recombine them for new activities. Outgrown toys in good condition should be given to a child the proper age. That is the best kind of recycling.

If you are missing pieces from your games, improvise. Use an inverted birthday candleholder as a playing piece, buttons to replace lost checkers. Combine spools, beads, and toy parts for chess pieces.

Make your own games from discards. For a toss game, attach foam cups to a large, inverted meat tray with paper fasteners and glue. Find some tossables (buttons, pennies). With your friends, take turns tossing.

Make bowling pins of bottles from detergent, shampoo, etc. (about 19- to 24-oz size). For each pin, pour some plaster into base, about 1/2" deep, to add weight. Or put some sand in the bottom. To prevent sand from spilling out, put glue inside top and screw on so that it won't open. Then cover top with masking tape. Use a wiffle or other plastic ball to bowl.

For a scoop ball game, cut top of a gallon bottle with handle. (See Plastic Bottles, p. 30, for cutting instructions.) Tie on a small ball. How many tries does it take to catch the ball in the scoop?

Or make two scoops without string. Play catch with a friend, using plastic scoops to catch and toss the ball back and forth to each other.

SCOOP BALL

THE EYES HAVE IT

MATERIALS

- Plastic cap about 3" in diameter and 1" deep
- Meat tray
- Markers
- Two black beads about 1/4" in diameter
- Paper punch
- Clear kitchen wrap

INSTRUCTIONS

1. Trace around cap on flat part of meat tray. Cut out just inside of the line so this disk will fit inside of cap. Punch two holes.

2. With marker, draw a face. Use punched out holes as eyes.

3. Glue face onto cap, add beads. Cover with clear wrap and tape in back.

The game: roll beads about until they land in the eyes.

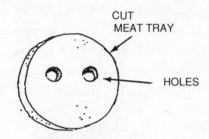

CUT MEAT TRAY

HOLES

1.

CAP

2.

3.

MINIATURES

Add to dollhouse decor using plastic discards. Cut meat trays to construct a stove or other kitchen appliances. To make any rectangular furniture, you can start with meat-tray pieces glued together and then add details. For the little accessories that make a miniature room look more homey, collect toothpaste and other tube tops, caps, and cosmetic bottle tops. Add beads and buttons as shown.

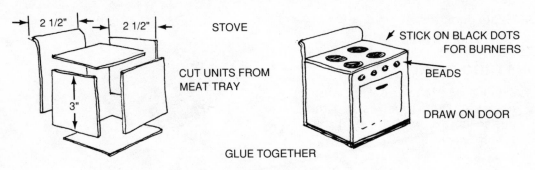

STOVE

CUT UNITS FROM MEAT TRAY

GLUE TOGETHER

STICK ON BLACK DOTS FOR BURNERS

BEADS

DRAW ON DOOR

MINIATURE ACCESSORIES

CANDLESTICKS

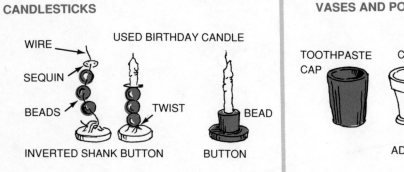

WIRE

USED BIRTHDAY CANDLE

SEQUIN

BEADS

TWIST

BEAD

INVERTED SHANK BUTTON

BUTTON

VASES AND POTS

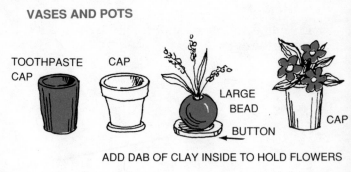

TOOTHPASTE CAP

CAP

LARGE BEAD

BUTTON

CAP

ADD DAB OF CLAY INSIDE TO HOLD FLOWERS

LAMP

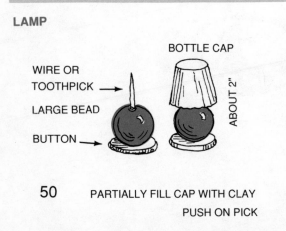

BOTTLE CAP

WIRE OR TOOTHPICK

LARGE BEAD

BUTTON

ABOUT 2"

50

PARTIALLY FILL CAP WITH CLAY
PUSH ON PICK

BOWLS AND DISHES

BUTTON WITH RIM

CONVEX BUTTON

PILL BOTTLE CAP

DISHES

1/2 OF CONTAINER FROM VENDING MACHINE

BUTTON

GLUE

SHANK BUTTON

COVER HOLES IN BUTTONS WITH SEQUINS OR PAPER DOTS

BRAIDED MINI RUG

MATERIALS

- Discarded panty hose
- Needle and thread

INSTRUCTIONS

1. Cut three strips of the nylon about 1 1/2" wide. Braid together. To lengthen braid, sew on new strips end to end so there is no lump, and continue braiding.

2. Shape braided strip into an oval, sewing it together as you make the coil. Press flat with a cool iron and pressing cloth. (Never put an iron directly onto nylon or it will melt.)

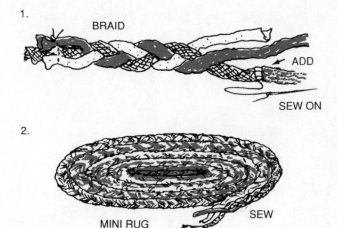

1. BRAID

ADD

SEW ON

2.

MINI RUG   SEW

TABLE FOR DOLLHOUSE

MATERIALS

- Plastic party wineglass base
- Clear pill bottle about 2 1/2" high
- Plastic piece cut from clear deli container
- Model glue

INSTRUCTIONS

1. Cut a circle of clear plastic slightly smaller than base of wineglass.

2. Glue together as shown (follow the instructions on the label).

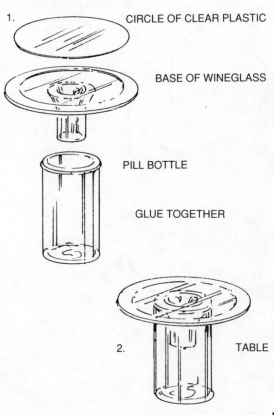

1. CIRCLE OF CLEAR PLASTIC

BASE OF WINEGLASS

PILL BOTTLE

GLUE TOGETHER

2.   TABLE

51

SPOOL ANIMALS

Spools from sewing thread are now made of plastic. They can make party favors or toys for a toddler.

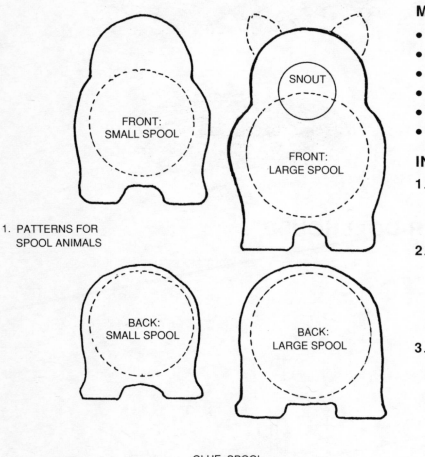

1. PATTERNS FOR SPOOL ANIMALS

FRONT: SMALL SPOOL

FRONT: LARGE SPOOL

SNOUT

BACK: SMALL SPOOL

BACK: LARGE SPOOL

MATERIALS

- Spool
- Meat tray
- Paint
- Glue
- Three small black beads
- String or rope

INSTRUCTIONS

1. Trace patterns onto flat part of meat tray. Cut out pieces and glue to each end of spool. Check that feet are level.

2. Cut 3/4" diameter snout from curved part of meat tray. Draw on mouth. Cut out appropriate-shaped ears. Cut off a piece of string or rope for tail. Glue on ears, snout, and tail. Paint. Glue on bead eyes and nose.

3. Make a menagerie of four-legged animals, a barnyard, or zoo. Some animals will need longer necks, horns, or larger snouts. Adjust patterns as necessary.

2.

GLUE SPOOL

3.

GIRAFFE   BULL

CUT TRUNK FROM MEAT TRAY

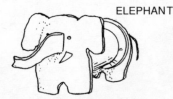

ELEPHANT

RACCOON

ART OF PLASTIC DISCARDS

Some great artists have made masterpieces out of discards. Use your talent and imagination to transform ordinary objects into art. It's fun!

In their studios, many artists find practical uses for discards. A meat tray makes a good palette. Paint keeps moist for days in a container with a snap-on lid. A discarded shower curtain protects work surfaces.

Squeeze bottles can be used to apply paint. Fill an empty roll-on deodorant bottle with paint to get unusual effects. Use an old toothbrush to spatter-paint.

SCULPTURE

Some sculptures are carved of one piece, others are a combination of many pieces. In making a sculpture, it is important to turn it and look at it from all sides as you work.

MATERIALS
- Plastic foam packing pieces
- Foam cups
- Wire clothes hanger (or old curtain rod or dowel)
- Interesting plastic pieces
- Thin wire
- Screws or bolts
- Glue

INSTRUCTIONS
1. Select a packing piece for the base. Cut a wire rod from a coat hanger. Insert into base. This wire rod (armature) is needed to hold units together and support added pieces.

PAINT BLACK

53

2. For center forms, stack some larger shapes of the packing pieces, then push onto armature. Add more wires at angles as needed to support the extra units.

3. Experiment with additions: see what looks good. Cut meat trays, slices of cups, pieces of plastic foam. Accentuate odd shapes already in place. Add caps, lids, straws, etc.

4. Glue together. Some additions may need special attachment. Staple or use wire or pipe cleaners to tie or lash pieces into place. Screws, bolts and nuts, paper fasteners are useful. Make a hole first in heavier plastics.

5. When all units are secured, look at your sculpture from all sides. Add more if needed. Cover screw heads with beads or sequins. Paint the base black, using latex or acrylic paint. Never use spray paints on plastic foam. Add dabs and swashes of color to tie elements together visually.

Of course, your sculpture will look totally different. It will be a creation determined by the plastic discards you have available and your imagination.

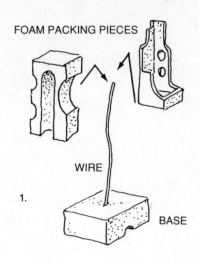

FOAM PACKING PIECES

1.

WIRE

BASE

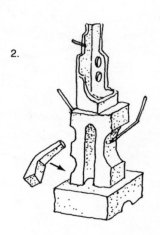

2.

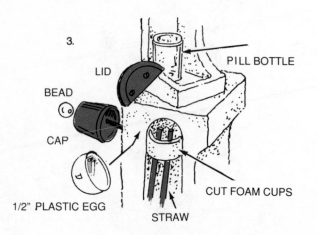

3.

PILL BOTTLE

LID

BEAD

CAP

1/2" PLASTIC EGG

STRAW

CUT FOAM CUPS

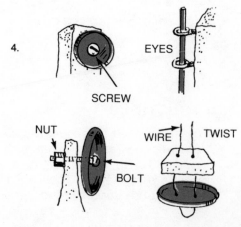

4.

EYES

SCREW

NUT

WIRE   TWIST

BOLT

BIRD MOBILE

MATERIALS

- Plastic foam meat trays (in colors if available)
- Snap-on lid
- Paper punch
- Paper for pattern
- Serrated kitchen paring knife
- Four-holed button
- Orange and black markers
- Nylon fishing line
- Ten black beads
- Needle
- Straight pin

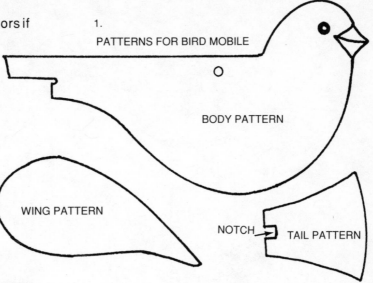

1.

PATTERNS FOR BIRD MOBILE

BODY PATTERN

WING PATTERN

NOTCH | TAIL PATTERN

INSTRUCTIONS

1. Trace patterns and cut out of paper. Place pattern for body on flat area of meat tray, avoiding embossed letters. Trace around. Place tail on slightly curved part of tray. Draw wing, turn pattern over, and draw other wing. Repeat, making five birds. With knife, cut out pieces. Trim any unevenness with scissors.

2. With markers, color and draw beak outlines. Draw eye, or glue on a bead for each eye. With needle, punch hole at top of back, as shown in pattern.

3. Cut five pieces of nylon line into various lengths from 5" to 15". Push one end of first line through hole on the bird. Tie securely. Glue tail on horizontally, sliding notch under body end. Glue on wings. Repeat for other four birds.

4. Hold up each bird by its line. If a bird tips wrongly (see drawing), remove its wings, and make new hole further up its body. Retie and replace wings.

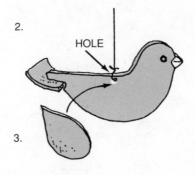

2.

HOLE

3.

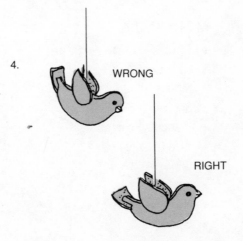

4.

WRONG

RIGHT

55

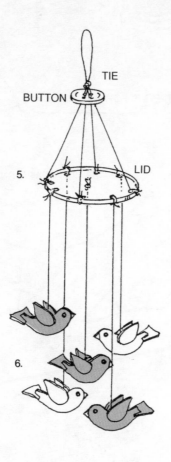

5. With the punch, make eight holes around edge of lid, spacing them somewhat evenly apart. With the pin, poke a tiny hole in center of lid. Push end of line from one bird up through center hole. Tie knot large enough not to pull out, and slide it against the lid.

6. Tie end of line from another bird to a hole in edge of lid. Repeat with the remaining birds, attaching to alternate holes around outside of lid.

To make top hanger, cut four 9" pieces of nylon line. Tie ends of each line through remaining holes on lid. Then bring each one up through the button, and tie them together above button. Knot ends together to make hanging loop. To hang evenly, adjust lines as needed. At the same time, check that birds hang at various heights. If not, adjust lengths of line. Hang up your mobile.

VARIATIONS

For an abstract mobile, cut random shapes of colorful plastic bottles, or use leftovers from other projects.

STAMP'EM NOTE CARDS

MATERIALS

- Plastic foam meat trays
- Stamp pad
- Markers
- Paper
- Pencil with eraser
- Vinyl eraser
- Glue
- Knife
- Nail
- Spool

56

1.

PRESS IN

PRINT

2.

MARKER ADDED

3.

4.

SPOOL

5.

CUT

6.

PRINT

INSTRUCTIONS

1. To make stamp, cut a 1 1/2" square out of meat tray. Plan design on paper. Draw it in reverse on the tray. With nail (or any pointed tool), press down the surface of each area to be white when printed.

2. Press stamp onto the stamp pad and press firmly onto scrap paper to see effect. Fix where needed and try again. Make several stamps to get the look desired. Make an animal's face white. After printing, add eyes and whiskers with marker.

3. If you would like your initials on the card, make a pattern of your initials on paper. Turn over to transfer, so they will be in reverse on meat tray piece.

4. To make the stamp easier to use, glue it to a spool that becomes a handle.

5. As a border design for your card, make a different kind of stamp, using a knife to cut a design into the edge of a vinyl eraser.

6. For note cards, cut paper and fold to the size needed. Create original designs combining your different

stamps; add borders, and initials if desired. Stamp on dots, by inking eraser end of pencil. Use markers to add color and details.

VARIATIONS

Decorate plain stationery with small design at top. Cut larger pieces, almost as large as stamp pad, for picture "prints" to be framed. To make gift wrap, draw guidelines on plain paper. Then stamp and repeat for all-over pattern.

GLOSSARY

Bacteria. Single-celled microscopic organisms. Some can cause disease; others break down solid waste.

Biodegradable. The ability of material to be broken down by organisms, such as bacteria; also, to be able to rot.

Convenience Foods. Foods that have been prepared and packaged for sale, such as frozen dinners or take-out foods, that need little or no cooking.

Curbside Recycling Program. The process in many communities of separating recyclables to be picked up by a recycling truck at our homes.

Degradable. The ability of a product to dissolve in a landfill, water, or in the air without harming the environment.

Dump. A place where discarded materials are left, often illegally. In most communities it is replaced by a sanitary landfill.

Environment. Our surroundings, including the air we breathe, the water we drink, and the land around us.

Garbage. Originally, waste food that was thrown away; now, any material that is unwanted. Also, trash, refuse, or municipal solid waste.

Hazardous. Dangerous to health.

Incinerator. A building where garbage and other waste materials are burned to create a smaller amount of solid waste in the form of ash.

Methane. An odorless, colorless, explosive gas often produced during the decomposition of solid wastes under conditions without oxygen. Sometimes it can be used as a fuel.

NIMBY. Stands for Not In My Back Yard. Negative attitudes about the building of prisons, airports, landfills, incinerators, and even recycling centers near one's home or in one's community.

Organism. Any living thing.

Photodegradable. The ability of material to break down when exposed to ultraviolet light from the sun.

Pollution. Contamination of earth, water, or air from chemicals, gases, or solid wastes.

Recyclable. The ability of a material (such as glass, aluminum, tin, iron, paper, plastic, and oil) to be reused.

Recycle. To collect and reprocess manufactured materials for reuse either in the same form or as part of a different product.

Recycling Center. A site where manufactured materials are collected and resold for recycling. If people bring recyclables directly to a center, it often is called a drop-off center; if they receive payment for the discards, it may be called a buy-back center.

Resource Recovery. Term used to describe the use of waste materials for conversion into fuel to generate electricity.

Reuse. To extend the life of an item by repairing or modifying it, or by creating new uses for it.

Sanitary Landfill. A site specially prepared for burial and decomposition of solid waste to reduce hazards to public health and safety.

Solid Waste. All garbage and trash, including household discards and industrial materials.

Solid Waste Management. The controlling, handling, and disposal of all garbage by a community.

Toxic. Poisonous.

FIND OUT MORE

In theory almost everything can be recycled, but in practice a lot depends on you and your community. Listed here are the most common items that can be recovered and recycled before they go into the solid waste stream:

Paper. Newspaper, books, magazines, office papers, commercial print, corrugated packaging, folding cartons, cardboard, bags

Glass. Beer/soda bottles, wine/spirits bottles, food containers

Metal. Ferrous metal (iron and steel), including food and beverage cans, appliances, automobiles, aluminum, including soda cans, lead (car batteries), other non-ferrous (such as copper and brass)

Plastic. Plates and cups, clothing and shoes, soft drink bottles, milk bottles, containers, bags, wraps

Rubber. Tires, clothing and shoes

Textiles and *Leather.* Clothing and shoes

Other Organic Material. Food, yard wastes, wood chips

Motor Oil.

Items not easily recyclable are oily rags, household batteries, paper mixed with food, disposable diapers, and other multi-material products that can't readily be separated into reusable materials.

A material is truly recyclable only if there is a recycling system in place. Successful recycling depends upon having the necessary technology to collect, sort, and process recoverable materials, as well as finding a market for them. Your community may be capable of providing programs for only a few of these items. To find recyclers outside your community, look in the yellow pages of a telephone directory under such headings as Recycling Centers, Waste Reduction, Waste Paper, Scrap Metal, etc., for businesses devoted to salvaging waste. However, it may not be economically wise to spend a lot of time and gasoline to find a far-off recycler. Your best bet is to promote and expand existing programs in your community.

We would like to acknowledge the following organizations for their help. They can provide you, too, with information to increase your knowledge and help you in your recycling efforts.

Companies and Organizations

America the Beautiful Fund
201 Shoreham Building
Washington, DC 20005
(202) 638-1649
Provides information on how to grow plants in plastic bags and how to make a "column" garden using plastic containers.

Browning-Ferris Industries
14701 St. Mary's
Houston, TX 77079
(713) 870-8100
(Also contact its regional offices)
Guide: *Mobius Curriculum: Understanding the Waste Cycle.*

Center for Plastics Recycling Research
Rutgers University
Building 3529, Busch Campus
Piscataway, NJ 08855
(201) 932-3683
Information Center open to the public.

Council for Solid Waste Solutions
1275 K St., NW, Suite 400
Washington, DC 20005
(202) 371-5319
(800)-2-HELP-90 for booklet: *How to Set Up a School Recycling Program.*

Illinois Department of Energy and Natural Resources
325 West Adams, Room 300
Springfield, IL 62704-9950
(217) 785-2800
Provides a variety of booklets, including a teacher's handbook, *Solid Waste: From Problems to Solutions.* Or write your own state environmental agency.

INFORM, Inc.
381 Park Ave. South
New York, NY 10016
(212) 689-4040

Institute for Local Self-Reliance
2425 18th St., NW
Washington, DC 20009
(202) 232-4108

Institute of Scrap Recycling Industries
1627 K St., NW, Suite 700
Washington, DC 20006
(202) 466-4050

Middlesex County Department of Solid Waste Management
100 Bayard St.
New Brunswick, NJ 08901
(908) 745-1470

National Audubon Society
950 Third Ave.
New York, NY 10022
(212) 832-3200
Newsletter: *Audubon Adventures*, special recycling issue.

National Consumers League
815 15th St., NW, Suite 516
Washington, DC 20005
(202) 639-8140
Booklet: *The Earth's Future is in Your Grocery Cart.*

National Solid Wastes Management Association
1730 Rhode Island Ave., NW, Suite 1000
Washington, DC 20036
(202) 659-4613
Booklet: *Meet Walt Wastenot.*

Plastic Bottle Institute
The Society of the Plastics Industry
1275 Connecticut Ave., NW, Suite 400
Washington, DC 20005
(202) 371-5200
Plastics Recycling Directory.

Polystyrene Packaging Council
1025 Connecticut Ave., NW
Washington, DC 20036
(202) 822-6424

The Proctor & Gamble Co.
One Proctor & Gamble Plaza
Cincinnati, OH 45202

Recycle America
Waste Management, Inc.
3003 Butterfield Rd.
Oak Brook, IL 60521
(708) 572-8878

Renew America
1400 16th St., NW, Suite 710
Washington, DC 20036
(202) 232-2252
Provides examples of successful recycling programs.

Solid Waste Information Clearing House (SWICH)
P.O. Box 7219
Silver Spring, MD 20910
(800) 67-SWICH
Funded by EPA, this is a one-stop source for solid waste information. They would like to hear from you about your recycling activities.

Scott Worldwide Foodservice
Scott Plaza I
Philadelphia, PA 19113
(800) 835-7268

United States Environmental Protection Agency (EPA)
Office of Solid Waste
Washington, DC 20460
(800) 424-9346
The federal agency will provide much information, including *Recycling Works!* and a list of state recycling contacts for every state, or contact the regional EPA branch nearest to where you live.

Wellman, Inc.
1040 Broad St., Suite 302
Shrewsberry, NJ 07702
(201) 542-7300
A major plastics recycler.

Successful School Programs

Help Our World
Mountain Park School
Berkeley Heights, NJ 07922
Contact: Rebecca Johnson
(201) 464-1713

Recycle 1,000
Silver Lake Elementary School
401 Webster
Bladen, NE 68928
Contact: Denise Koch
(402) 756-1311

Students Tackle Ocean Plastic
Ocean City Elementary School
Ocean City, MD 21842
Contact: Sandra Hornung
(301) 289-6800/6531

Further Reading

Other *How on Earth* books published by The Millbrook Press:

How on Earth Do We Recycle Glass? by Joanna Randolph Rott and Seli Groves.

How on Earth Do We Recycle Metal? by Rudy Kouhoupt with Donald B. Marti, Jr.

How on Earth Do We Recycle Paper? by Helen Jill Fletcher and Seli Groves.

Buy Now, Pay Later! Smart Shopping Counts by Thompson Yardley (Brookfield, CT: The Millbrook Press, 1992).

50 Simple Things Kids Can Do to Save the Earth by J. Jauna (Kansas City, MO: Andrews and McMeel, 1990).

Going Green: A Kid's Handbook to Saving the Planet by John Elkington, Julia Hailes, Douglas Hill, and Joel Makower (New York: Viking Penguin, 1990).

Recycling Plastic, by Judith Condon (New York, Franklin Watts, 1991).

Re/Uses: 2,133 Ways to Recycle and Reuse the Things You Ordinarily Throw Away by Carolyn Jabs (New York: Crown Publishers, 1982).

What a Load of Trash! Rescue Your Household Waste by Steve Skidmore (Brookfield, CT: The Millbrook Press, 1991).

INDEX

ABOUT THE AUTHORS

Janet Potter D'Amato is an accomplished craftswoman who, with her husband Alex, has produced many craft books. In the past 20 years, she has created, written, or illustrated over 50 children's books.

A designer of new crafts or new applications of old crafts, she focuses on saving and reusing recyclable materials.

Janet and her husband, who live in Bronxville, New York, have two daughters and two grandsons.

Laura Stephenson Carter is a free-lance journalist who specializes in science and environmental reporting. She is an active volunteer at a nature preserve.

She and her husband live in Short Hills, New Jersey, with their two young daughters.